Single Stream

Eyes of the Master

MysterE

Book XI

THE ANCIENTS FOLLOWED
THEIR HEARTS TO BUILD
ENLIGHTENED SOCIETY,
WHILE THE REST PLAYED
MUSICAL CHAIRS.

 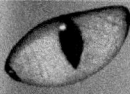

WHEN THE MUSIC STOPPED
THE GAME WAS DONE AND
ALL HAD LOST BUT ONE,
THE ANCIENTS WELCOMED
EVERYONE HOME.

Single Stream: Eyes of The Master

By MysterE

Copyright © 2025 by Mr. E. Dan Smith III

All rights reserved.
This book may not be reproduced in whole or
in part without written permission from the publisher, except by a
reviewer who may quote brief passages in a review; nor may any part of
this book be copied, stored in a retrieval system, or transmitted in any
form or means, without written permission
from the publisher.

Library of Congress: Data Available

ISBN: **979-8-218-64240-2**

Publisher: EASEup Life is Heart in Sedona, AZ 86336

Editorial: E
Photography: E

Absolutely No Artificial Intelligence.
Agent444.com

Acknowledgements

This book is dedicated is Keeley J Brand, my extraordinary compadre who reminds me in the most not-obvious ways, who I am – and in the most obvious ways, who I am not. For how does anyone truly know themselves, but in a perfect mirror?

Also to my father E. Dan Smith II, Sue, Ava, Anya, Eliza, Alden, Elizabeth, Billy, Carlos, Bill, Paul, Mac, TD, Tavon, Donna, Michael, Edward, Mark, Liana, Deborah, Reese, Ross, Wendy, Lucie, Rhonne, Vale, Amanda, GG, Lina, Heidi, Angee, Habib, Matthew, Mike, Kim, Bob, Kristina, Kerani, Allan, Sadarshan, Debra Mae, Dosi, Christian, Gretchen, Linda, Craig, PJ, Paul, Chief, Meera, Corey, Chloe, Jimy, Corwin, Sharon, Andy, Niki, Meg, Amy, Sandika, Juan, Paul, Dani, Andre, Greg, Cov, Matt, Clay, Robert, Tony, Clark, Miller, Elizabeth, Victoria, Enrique, Dina, Massood, Meghan, Colleen, Susie, Jonathon, Jimmy, Johnny, Nara, Jai, James, Flo, George, Joshua, Adam, Sabil, and to all angels we met on our journey through Mexico and the US. Each of you played a significant role. Thank you.

Also, to Vickie Champion, for helping me make sense of the senseless.

And, Single Stream certainly could not have happened without our Monday Night Zoom Class regulars, Michael, Mike, Sean, Ivan, James, Aaron, Curtis, Jeremy, and the others who have participated since 2020.

One final note: For Gene, who lived the Ancient Way. Thank you for the demonstration. We know you are smiling.

Table of Contents

Part One: Inspiration

Chapter I   **1** - *Setting the Stage*
Chapter II   **5** - *A Glimpse of the Infinite*

Part Two: The Problem

Chapter III   **11** - *Knowledge of the Ordinary*
Chapter IV   **23** - *Wisdom in the Obvious*
Chapter V   **39** - *Demonstration of Possibility*

The Bridge

Chapter VI   **51** - *It is Already Done*

Part Three: The Solution

Chapter VII   **73** - *Down By the River*
Chapter VIII   **85** - *Planting Seeds*
Chapter IX   **89** - *MisCreation*
Chapter X   **105** – *Sitting in the Stream*

Extras:

113 - The Ball of Light
117 - Other Books by MysterE
119 - Heart Rocks
120 - Glossary

Part One
Inspiration

I - *Setting the Stage - 1*
II - *A Glimpse of the Infinite - 5*

Chapter I
Setting the Stage

Why does something simple require 18,000 words?

I invite you patiently to read every word, and I'm grateful you will. This book is lifetimes of work, put into one little package.

Stay with it. We start with a short journey, then introduce the material before heading on a bigger journey, and lastly, finish with something we must see. When complete, we are changed.

There was no aim with this book beforehand. I'm not privy to the substance or the timeline. Suddenly, information arrives, and in a few weeks, it is together.

The material is repetitive. Keep going, until a distillation happens in you. My job is simply to formulate and put into a construct, words that free the mind and open the heart. It takes all my focus, and then when the book is done being written, it releases me. Then I release it "as is" without formal editing or proofreading.

For all of us, it is becoming more challenging to stay above the drama and chaos of change. Therefore, we must learn to master surfing waves of change, by giving up ideas about formality.

Sometimes grieving is all we require to shift. Once we give ourselves permission to weep with joy rather than in sorrow, we see how one frees us, and one binds us. In this, we learn to grieve and feel deeply, knowing we can only advance.

My invitation is thus: Take your time. Read the book and be guided. It is about slowing down amidst fast-paced change to access your inner guide and become what wants to happen.

In stillness, the anomalies of life sparkle. When you notice something odd or strangely out of place, sit with the occurrence to investigate. When you know its truth, reality shifts. Pay attention as it relates to your experience of this book.

In our quest for the Grail, we must learn to let *all* decisions make themselves.

Patience gives us access to true power. We must see that when we are making decisions, they cannot be right. That we, in our human vision, only make wrong choices. In this way, we can be open for accelerated evolutionary change by slowing down to the speed of change itself. In our alignment we realize, choices are illusionary.

Timing then, plays a significant role, for when we are diligent and allow decisions to be made for us, it signals we have released limitation by investigating a new relationship with God, and how we utilize time.

This is what we want; to be led into choiceless choices by making no choices, except to let them happen.

When we are peaceful, this is obvious. The next door is always open. If we are elsewhere in our quest; indecision, impatience or judgment, we skip right on past the doorway and thus, return to this lesson, repeatedly, until we can be still and recognize God within.

In the book, *there are italics*. Read the *italics* aloud twice with feeling. While the narrative is focused on the collective, referencing "we" and "us," periodically the focus becomes "you." This is the way it arrived. Enjoy seeing something new.

Chapter II
A Glimpse of the Infinite

In spiritual awakening, everything turns back into itself and awakens as One. Period.

It can be very confusing and quite frankly should be confusing because what thought it separated from God, did not and is returning to origin.

Imagine two rivers coming down two different canyons that are bound to meet up, only one doesn't know it yet.

It's exhilarating as the other canyon comes into view. The sound of water crashing and splashing onto the banks. The unknown is rushing towards us. First contact ignites a blossoming desire to dive deeper as we experience the knowledge of something new.

We Gain a Glimpse of the Infinite

Then a jostling. Our world is changing quickly, and our familiarity is challenged. Our arguments with reality are fruitless. There is no going backward now, as we are disturbed into an awakening by the turbulence of interweaving waters as we begin to merge to become the wisdom of something new.

In the merging, then joining, we become concerned about our identity and what is going to happen to us. There is a panic perhaps, of losing ourselves and our importance. We do nt yet realize the ocean ahead, and how fruitless our conditioned attempts are, for self-preservation.

This assimilation is coming for us all. We are being ushered into a *demonstration of something new*. But how?

Every person's journey of spiritual awakening is unique, and at times, it seems there are no prescriptions that satisfy the symptoms of an (in)voluntary vast sweeping change of mind.

Yet one choice changes the immediate trajectory of our lives. We only have one choice to make, and it is to have a happy outcome to every scene, play and act in the theatrical performance of our lives. All other choices are not choices at all, but delay tactics to this choice. For until we surrender our argument with reality, we will remain in conflict.

It's therefore essential for each of us to choose a joyful journey in life by connecting to *Single Stream* or 'we' consciousness.

To choose happiness in all experience, is to bring our life force energy under conscious control, allowing our thoughts, words and deeds to be guided by Divine Inspiration. The outcome of life then becomes compassion.

This book, *Single Stream* is an ethereal instruction manual for the correct use of energy in thought, language, action, sexuality and commerce to ignite divine inspiration in the coming New Earth by diving headfirst into the living waters of God.

For when thought, word and deed are aligned with the heart, they are stronger than ocean currents. Anything becomes possible through our demonstration of wisdom.

> We are being invited to shift from:
> *What is happening to me?* Into:
> ***What wants to happen for us?***

Single Stream   8   *Eyes of the Master*

Part Two
The Problem

III – *Knowledge of the Ordinary - 11*
IV – *Wisdom in the Obvious - 23*
V – *Demonstration of Possibility - 39*

Chapter III
Knowledge of the Ordinary

The Meek Shall Inherit New Earth

Despite what everybody else is doing, now is not the time to **try to carve** out a piece of the pie. The idea of success is quickly outdating itself. In truth, now is the time to go exactly in the opposite direction.

An awakened person's demonstration is to live the only true occupation: There is no more essential walk on Earth than to offer the knowledge and wisdom one has experienced to assist others along *the Way*.

One doesn't do it for money, fame or importance – only for the true satisfaction gained from sharing in the way God prescribes.

To put it another way - when the heart is awakened, a process of purification is underway. Resistance is insanity. Acceptance becomes peace.

Satisfaction

The byproduct of what we 'do' for a living, suddenly doesn't matter. The scale or the product of our investment in the world is no longer measured by the same criteria.

Our satisfaction becomes simply demonstrating compassion; knowing when we are agreeable to our hearts, everything we require to thrive in life falls into place with ease and grace.

We learn *satisfaction* is a byproduct of listening within and acting solely upon inspiration, which guides our lives efficiently and peacefully. Satisfaction then, cannot be manufactured in the world any longer.

Satisfaction is the yield of unwavering faith, certainty and devotion to the mantra of New Earth, *All is Provided for Now*.

New Earth

The New Earth is the Earth we live upon, without our addiction, as seen through Eyes of the Master. It is a perfect environment of natural law.

Our Addiction

The addiction we all face, by virtue of our birth, is not to a substance, habit or indulgence – it is addiction to an unnatural thought system of conflict, and the dramatic debris fields that ensue.

Conflict is a human invention. The only way out of this conditioning is to expunge the root cause of the addiction itself, for false cannot grow in truth.

This total reversal of our thought processes is withdrawal. It is more a transmutation of energy than a regurgitation, and the process can feel like complete insanity.

Albeit temporary insanity: For the less we resist and argue with change, the shorter and less pronounced is the insanity.

Ultimately, conflicting streams of thought are replaced by the Divine Mind in surrender. We call this *Single Stream*.

Single Stream

In the Stream there are no conflicting thoughts.
In the Stream the thought of 'not enough' does not exist.
In the Stream there is only peace, health and abundance.
In the Stream we are in communion with God's thoughts.

When in alignment with the pure presence of awareness in Single Stream, we experience neither conflict nor scarcity.

God's Thoughts

God's thoughts always unify.
God's thoughts are simple, clear and feel light in the heart.
God's thoughts inspire, uplift and are healing.
God's thoughts are accessible through intuition.

Listening to God's thoughts, leads us to our Master Blueprint role to assume true responsibility for our lives.

Divine Blueprints

God's plan is the Master Blueprint, a mosaic of Divine Blueprints. Everyone has a Divine Blueprint.

The Divine Blueprint is your single unique spiritual journey reflective in the pattern of the Master Blueprint. We are each a facet of an infinite mandala of divine perfection. As a Spark of the Divine, we each have a purpose to fill and are essential to the whole.

And we will fill our purpose, for this is God's plan.

Life is more enjoyable when I accept God's plan.

Divine Blueprints are energy fields that channel light and matter into form, according to the image of itself, much like blueprints of a building, or DNA.

God is the architect, and I am <u>the finished product</u>.

A finished product so beautiful and essential, we would halt everything in our lives to rest simply in the awe and majesty of ourselves.

By simply withdrawing our human self-involvement, (thinker and doer), we would see the perfection of God's plan already in play and recognize:

My only objective here is to polish my lens and truly see.

Truly seeing would immediately recognize both disparity in our potential (God's plan,) and simple solutions for our human play on Earth today.

We would see our addiction to conflict in the constant argument we have with God's Reality, and we would see how we justify this conflict through separated thoughts.

Separated Thoughts

Any thought conditional, divisional, judgmental, competitive or hierarchical. Separated thoughts are secretive, myopic, complex, and serious. They depress, belittle and justify.

By entertaining separated thoughts, we create suffering with the conflict we invent, and then by blaming others, even God – we further cover our lens of awareness with shame and guilt. Our self-delusion is multilayered, multigenerational and yet, not of us.

Sustained Effort

We have been sold we live in prosperity, freedom and peace. Yet our movies, news and entertainment glorify war and disparity. With nuclear missiles pointed in every direction, we watch, pretending not to notice we are the characters we see, and live in someone else's, scripted fantasy.

What we have left of our treasure, is slipping into more conflict. Our technological advancement has not brought simplicity – life is more complex as our attention is harvested by compounding streams of thought, threats and media.

>Fragmented attention = a fragmented reality.

>*Are we really that surprised?*

Fragmentation

The practices we have relied on to stabilize; religion, success and self-help have become ineffective. Peace is more elusive as we realize the depth of the seduction. We are reliant on a broken system for direction and validation. Our crossroads is now a roundabout. Do we fold or go all in? Neither is a good option.

Now seeing our addiction, withdrawal seems unfathomable.

Depth of Seduction

> ** Whatever I give my attention,*
> *I join with my will.*

A sobering thought - perhaps enough to create a disturbance to jar us from the illusion. Read it twice. *

Every text, voice mail, reel and film. Every show, date, website, conversation, song, glance and class. All monetary transactions and services rendered. All thought, word and deed.

Read it a third time. *

As soon as we recognize self-deception with our human eyes, we will desire to see through *the Master's Eyes*.

With this renewed determination, anything becomes possible. We can see fragmentation then, as sparking a mass awakening of our collective heart. A rebirthing of a yearning to keep the sacred alive amidst the quickening. Naturally, we birth a dedication to live in balance with all.

Therefore, to become sober, we must first initiate and cultivate a powerful desire to be free of the conditioned mind. By remaining in a mental resistance field larger than our desire field, we remain *unknowingly* seduced. We are not only lost. We have forgotten we are lost.

Resistance Field

A secretive mind of separated thoughts, cut off from the Divine.

Symptoms: Not enough, fearful, impatient, unforgiving, sick, possessive, shameful, depressed, manic, confused, lethargic, unworthy, jealous, conspiring, suspicious, arrogant and lustful for money, power, fame, status, and sex. A low vibration.

Desire Field

A clear and present mind with an open heart.

Symptoms: Peaceful, faithful, certain, curious, co-creative, harmonious, inclusive, enthusiastic, celebratory, devoted, generous, simple and compassionate. A high vibration.

It is with our heart then; we enable *True Vision*.

When we cultivate our desire <u>to love no matter what</u> or simply to know God: inspiration leads to breakthrough.

When we desire something, we initiate creative flow. Things start happening and we enjoy the ride. We naturally invest in expansion until our desire overwhelms the resistance.

This *love no matter what* becomes the measure of renewed faith and certainty. Desire becomes our untouchable superpower. We increase and direct our desire to know God and love all the way through resistance, with determination. We are glad for this. Only good can happen now. We have become catalyst agents for change.

'To love no matter what' means I have accepted: I am not the architect of change. We are not, only because our human vision cannot see the proper correction to make. We become more willing then - to accept God's outcome.

God's outcome could only be perfect, and better than mine. Rather than wasting energy on fruitless correction, the most efficient route must be purification.

Purification

Purification is simple. We keep adding pristine living waters of Single Stream to our discordant thought patterns, until we are completely free of the poison.

Single Stream is a vertical stream of energy moving up from the Earth through the feet, up the legs into the spine, traveling through the heart and expanding above the crown. It is a vortex and bends back into itself.

Much like how we throw sticks into a stream and watch them disappear, we can discard separated thoughts into the Stream for purification. We can flush our tears and release our fears.

A strong mind discards separated thoughts.
A strong mind uses memory to reveal who to pardon.
A strong mind invests in compassion.

A weak mind invests in conflict.

Desire - The Only Way

I am not being punished. I am being rewarded.

The reward is peace. In our communion with Single Stream, we discover there is more to the world we see. We are being summoned to give birth to something new within: *I desire to know myself through the Eyes of the Master and fulfill my destiny. What does it feel like to know God's love?*

The desire to know God is the only mechanism by which valuable interpersonal change can happen. It is the only measure of true satisfaction this world offers. A devotion in daily practice and activities to know who we truly are, is the only cure of our addiction to conflict.

It's almost too obvious to point out.

The conditioned thought system is so pervasive and dense, we believe it to be true. *I always get what I believe.*

We then justify fighting to protect a system of conflict and indulgence. *I always get what I tolerate.*

So obvious it is now - we live on a planet of exaggeration, consumption, war, scarcity and drama portrayed in mainstream media – and all investment of our time and attention in such, can only render more of the same.

Upon even further observation, we see it more clearly:

The whole play is plainly ordinary – lacking any true creativity. It's quite unfulfilling and hasn't any genuine substance at all.

On a planet of abundance, we manufactured scarcity.
With our intelligence, we have become dumb.
In a school of love, we have mastered war.
Certainly, there must be another way.
But how can we know the way?
We require Way-Showers.

The Order of the Black Sheep?

Chapter IV
Wisdom in the Obvious

Way-Showers

Way-Showers are those who walked ahead and have returned with good news: "Come this way. We have nothing to fear when we walk the way of our inner guidance. Our destiny is fantastical beyond our wildest dreams."

Way-Showers cover great distances and chart *the Way*, so all can travel more efficiently in less time. Our mission is to share our unique experience as a part of a great school of higher learning which serves as a gateway to another realm of existence here. The only curriculum is Love.

The curriculum demands we embrace life to see that people are not wrong or bad, but our conditioning is wrong, causing us to see incorrectly. And we are glad this thought system is wrong, and happy how we thought about the world and ourselves was a misinterpretation. *Whew! The entire thought system is wrong, it isn't about success, or failure, or me at all.*

In seeing our innocence, we release the conditioning and keep the truth of us intact.

It was wrong to judge, control and capitalize extravagantly.
It was wrong to belittle and bully with our complicity.
It was wrong to indulge and medicate excessively.
It was wrong to blame and lie compulsively.
Yet, we were wrong only in human sight.
Our only choices were confusion.

And in seeing we were in a wrong thought system: We are free to learn something new. We can cry our last tears and feel our last hurts.

Our tears are a weeping with joy for the clearing of our vision, rather than for being lost in confusion.

The Earth School of Love

Earth is the most advanced Mastery School in the Universe.

When One graduates, one goes beyond the Earth we see now. A peaceful exit appears when the learning is complete, and we remain here, as Way-Showers.

Completing the curriculum means transcending the obvious and ordinary human realms to become compassionate and empowered in love. In our triumph, we discover everything has been made new again.

We had been so myopically focused on our conditioned selves; it was impossible to recognize the truth. We are each far more than we have experienced. And there is far more to explore on Earth than our five senses report.

Our true nature is so magnificent, we plainly see: "Oh, how advanced are humans in the manufacturing of suffering, and how utterly ridiculous the whole notion is in truth."

I can learn suffering is not real. It's only an experience and it's a very small experience in the endless chain of now moments we call lives. We learn to see: *My separation is as voluntary, as the thoughts, I think.*

We discover in Earth School, we already have the faculty to operate with a capacity which can never lose, so there is never any risk in following our heart.

Thank you, Jesus Christ. Yes Jesus, for He demonstrated eyes are God's creative force.

And like a true Way-Shower, He shares His mastery. We each naively inherited the Master's Eyes.

Eyes of the Master

God is perfect creation, and perfect love.
God only sees wholeness and perfection.
Master Jesus sees with God's True Vision.

True Vision

True Vision is the creative force of the Universe.
True Vision alchemizes all into wholeness and perfection.
True Vision replicates in the image and likeness of God.

Though the Master never left us - in the evolving story of Christ's impact - the 2nd Coming appears unfulfilled. Yet now, is now the time. Now, it is of us, to realize the gift of sight, like Jesus did. We can accept the gift. *Actually, I simply forgot; I inherited the gift of sight.*

In Single Stream, we reconnect with our ability to heal and unify with God's True Vision.

True Vision turns life from a maze - into a labyrinth.

Mazes (Which Way?)

In a maze are multiple choice points and separate routes. "Do I go this way or that way?" In the mind of separated thoughts, our personal world is a maze.

There are dead ends and multiple entrances. The function of a maze is dualistic: To create <u>and</u> resolve the conflict of being lost, repeatedly.

For a maze to exist, our belief system must include the notion of free will. Yet again we are wrong. We are glad to be wrong.

Our separated thoughts made the maze <u>and</u> then generated conflict by constantly changing the maze.

No matter what 'improvements' we make, the maze remains a maze. Human free will to solve the maze must be an illusion. This is our seduction: If we believe we can win or lose; we remain in duality. Our belief in the maze causes it to be true.

Separated thoughts create external conflict, meaning we also see with flawed vision. Flawed vision cannot see how to establish correction in a flawed system. Flaws create flaws.

It is far simpler then, to vacate the entire system of conflicting thought than to attempt to fix us, or the system – especially when nothing is wrong.

And nothing is ever wrong in a labyrinth.

Labyrinths (*The Way*)

A labyrinth is one path, a *Single Stream*.

Labyrinths have a designated path. There are no choice points, except to notice. There is but one clear path, with twists and turns, yet there is only one step forward. A labyrinth is simpler.

In a labyrinth, one cannot argue with *the Way*. One simply follows along. *Strategy and cleverness are useless, on a one-way journey to the center of a predetermined route.*

The center represents the awakening of our heart; the place of nothing and everything. *Not knowing becomes knowledge and experience, wisdom.* The bindi or zero point in a Yin Yang.

Turning at the center of the labyrinth, the return represents the demonstration of our awakening for those we encounter.

The Yin Yang

Our free will: Do we walk a maze (96) or a labyrinth (69)?

In a Yin Yang, there is equal light and dark unfolding into one creative dance of balance, then folding back into itself again. We can struggle with duality or embrace its paradox.

96 Way – The Maze

96 Way is to operate with misinterpretation and reactivity, misguided by perception. To struggle in cyclical conflicts by arguing with life. On 96, we forget we are in God's Universe and superimpose separated thoughts upon natural law instead.

With our wrong thoughts, we project our maze of conditioning into life. Then we damn the creativity of it all, not realizing our error of introducing more conflict. We create rules and punish for order.

We think things like; "Life is unfair and should be different. Others can act or be different than they are now."

96 is learning through contrast by confusing the correct order of awareness. We make the conditioned mind our master and ignore our heart. Our point of awareness then, is from the dark. We cannot see in the dark.

96 is complexity. 96 is perception.

69 Way – The Labyrinth

69 Way is to live in balance and harmony, accepting life as always presenting the next step ahead as we walk in certainty and faith - knowing we couldn't be anywhere else, nor could we be anyone else, nor could we even be separate from God. Nor could our fellow inhabitants on Earth.

We reflect and heal to establish order.

69 is marked by an agreeability with life, a curiosity of learning and a willingness to follow the choices that feel right. When the mind plays role of servant, an exalted heart opens and intuition blossoms. All choice becomes choiceless.

Choiceless Choices

When the heart is open and the mind is silent, we align with destiny, and our next steps become obvious. We are no longer thinking; we feel enthusiasm and a peaceful knowing. This is the confirmation we are on our evolutionary track.

Now, we can see. Our focus becomes *Making Light of the Dark*.

69 is simplicity.
69 is visionary.

Different is the Same

Paradoxically, both ways 69 & 96 lead to God or master awareness. One is efficient, and one less so.

Furthermore, ***Ways 69 & 96 are the same path.***

Whichever path we find ourselves, it is certain we created it with our vision. Likewise, it is also certain we can immediately adjust perspective by merely shifting our point of awareness.

From our resistance field (mind) we travel 96. From our desire field (heart) we travel 69. Our sight creates our experience of the path we travel. The only path in existence.

Am I in conflict with my one path, or at peace?

The peaceful are in Single Stream, exercising the only free will: *Alignment with the Divine Blueprint.* This agreeability opens the Eyes of the Master.

True Vision changes the assemblage point of our awareness. It is no longer oriented from the dark. We see no conflict. Our reality ceases to confuse us, because without conflicting thoughts, natural order becomes evident.

Our point of awareness has become steady and balanced. Our reality returns to a peaceful state.

Neutrality

To see correctly, we must have a *neutral* experience with our conditioned mind, so separated thoughts have both permission and a pathway to vacate.

We can say: *If I'm not happy, I must be in the wrong mind. I have no more use for that!*

We might also say: *Why am I seeing unhappiness in others? I must be in the wrong thought system!*

Neutrality is the quality of the heart and of center of the Yin Yang. The center vibrates with the quality of nothingness; it the melding point of dark and light, masculine and feminine, and positive and negative.

Neutrality is the expression of surrender - our free will. In the heart we become comfortable in not knowing, and joyful with the continued expression of life as it happens.

Here 69 and 96 merge into *the Way*.

Our vision has been corrected, we see the one and only path that has always been.

>Our Free Will:
>*Go along with the Blueprint, or not.*
>*We are all returning to God.*

Free Will

We have a simple and plain choice that frees us.

By accepting we have been marionettes – and no one could have taken a different route because all have been in a maze of limitation - everyone receives a pardon and is exonerated from all wrongdoing.

The Knowledge: We each experience what we create through our vision. This is our lesson plan. Our collective experience is the result of collective seeing. Conditioned sight can only be wrong and will never lead us home. It is our acceptance of *seeing falsely cannot be real*, and our gladness to see the error, that allows for something new to be born.

The Wisdom: We are that powerful. Our thoughts are made manifest. *My vision gives all thoughts life.* We are all creators and perpetuate the attributes of the reality we believe we see.

Multiple thought streams create conflict and chaos. Single Stream does not. There has always been only one path, we simply misinterpreted reality. We were all misguided, and we can choose differently now.

We might say:

> *Wow, Everyone is Responsible and No One is at Fault.*
> *This means: There is nothing to forgive!*

The Demonstration: Seeing all people as innocent by being neutral, opinionless and withdrawn from all meaning of separated thoughts… while listening to the heart and following the inner guide, in surrender.

Surrender aligns us with God's plan, placing us squarely on the path of life purpose. Here, we find satisfaction in our devotion to compassionate creation.

The only way out is through - the Master's Eyes.

If I am for or against anything, I give it authority.
If I am neither for nor against, I am neutral.
Nothing can stick to me in neutrality.
Nothing unreal can frighten me.
No mistake can seduce me.
No occurrence can startle me.
I am never under control of others.
I can change my thoughts about anything.
Neutrality is how I bend time for advancement.

How Advancement Happens

All imbalance reflects scarcity. Scarcity is created by separated thinking, meaning all problems are symptoms of being not enough, or too much – or more simply, being disconnected from God. We must see through the illusion of separate problems and solve the only problem.

One Problem Only

Our only problem is our separated thinking: "I am (sick,) I can get (sick,) I am this body, something is wrong with me…"

These symptoms are a gift in that they reveal the error.

Separated thoughts sell us a vision of a closed system, separate from God and fearful. When we buy this offer, we make it true. When we believe the illusion, we experience separation as a false reality.

Whether an imbalance in sexuality, health, intoxicants, relationship dynamics or financial challenges – Our struggle reveals exactly what we believe and gives us the only effective recourse: Choose a joyful journey with a determination to love.

The Way is being rooted in willingness to learn the lessons of love in wholeness, rather than to argue with reality through conflict. *The Way* is the acceptance of true responsibility.

Willingness

It is our willingness to look at life opposite the way of our conditioning that allows for *the Way*. We might contemplate*; I see how I invested into conflict unknowingly, and how the returns are not of wholeness, nor to my liking. Perhaps there's a better way. I am willing, in my determination, to see.*

The Way is curious: *How is this (illness) a reflection of my separated thoughts? Could I be inquisitive about my symptoms rather than self-condemning and welcome this (illness) as a gift? How can I release the outcome to God and be happy?*

The reversal of thought allows us to feel. When we feel, we heal the heart which naturally corrects our sight, bit by bit.

We might then say to ourselves: *I appreciate this opportunity to learn, as I'm beginning to see when I appreciate everyone, even the suffering, judgment is jettisoned. Without judgment, I see a different landscape. I feel better in my devotion to life.*

Now I feel how life always supports me, and I've simply been in the wrong thought system! I'm so happy to see this system - in which I've been mired – is false. I thought it was real, but it is not. Therefore, I lay down having to be right and celebrate devoting myself to learn the lessons of love.

And, in vacating wrong thoughts, I see that I do not retain the "capacity to judge." Now I am more lighthearted and less controlling. I desire to learn the lesson of playfulness to see new opportunities on the pathway I could not see before.

And holy wow! Because now I see but one path, I realize I created lots of choices - imaginary choices - in my addiction to the illusionary. In fact, I spent a ridiculous amount of energy and time trying to figure out life, rather than simply living. Now I can experience what is meant for me.

Imagine

Thoughts direct vision:
Separated thoughts direct vision into
fragmentation, disease, scarcity & complexity.
Unifying thoughts reveal wholeness and simplicity.

Bodies, businesses, relationships, environments all reveal
beliefs as symptoms of separate thought accordingly. Energy
is neutral and follows instructions to replicate into experience.

We thought we could fail, get or be hurt, sacrifice and suffer.
We were wrong about being wrong. We were wrong about
everything. It was the thought system. Not us, ever. And
because of a wrong mind, there is nothing to forgive.

There were no other choices, but to discover:
The power to create follows our sight.
Realizing power is to accept
awesome responsibility.

We each have *the Eyes of Master*.
What we bless with our sight flourishes.
From what we withdraw sight, diminishes.

God does everything through our vision.
Our job is to be the finished product.

Thy Will Be Done.

Chapter V
Demonstration of Possibility

We only deceive ourselves with human eyes. This is wonderful wisdom. Now, only good can happen.

No matter what history, religious text or spiritual methodology we've studied, it is impossible for a separated mind to accurately relay significance through perception.

However, spiritual significance cannot change.

There is freedom then, in taking the spirit of the word, rather than rational understanding. In the heart, our discernment is focusing on what feels right, which gives the mind a backseat. We can observe rather than figure, allowing a transmission of awareness, for an evolutionary shift. Learning becomes an expression of feeling warm in the heart, and at peace.

Now we can study, listen and experience with a broader perspective, gaining the nectar of what advances us spiritually and leaving perception behind. We learn to trust where and with whom we are being led, by following the heart.

The Spiritually Advanced

Way-Showers are tapped into Single Stream, not more gifted.

Way Showers see how human vision fragments *one problem* into multiple fronts of conflict. The *one problem* is: Tolerance of a separated thought system, or disconnection from God.

In Single Stream, all streams of religion, background, belief and experience flow into One.

It doesn't matter which tributary one remembers taking, and to what effect. Every stream eventually enters the One Stream, where all individual strands are braided and unified in light.

In Single Stream, we travel beyond division into True Reality.

We are happy to learn:
We lose nothing, but sacrifice.
Anything espousing conflict is not true.
What does not illumine the heart has no value.

Giving Up All Battles at Once

We will never find peace through conflict. When we realize conflict is of wrong thoughts, we recalibrate, automatically.

Seeing the solution as solving one problem, rather than attempting to fix multiple symptoms of that problem, becomes the way of accelerated change. All battles then are resolved by communing with Single Stream. This initiates purification. Correction is now naturally underway.

Hold the Vision and Trust the Process

The process may become messy. It might get confusing. It might test everything you think you know. However, with Eyes of the Master, we see folly in chaos, learn lessons efficiently, and move beyond glad for the experience.

Jesus appeared to suffer in the crucifixion through our human eyes, for that is the nature of human vision. Though Jesus did not suffer, for he saw with the Master's Eyes.

Humanity sees suffering. Masters do not.

How one pair of Master's Eyes impacted humanity is a work in progress as seen by human sight. In this demonstration, Jesus Christ's legacy is often seen as, not enough.

Now then, is the time for all Children of God to accept Christ's True Vision as a testament to the individual essential purposes of our lives. *I can do what the Master does. It is arrogance to believe otherwise. We are all enough.*

Without separated thoughts, we cannot retain separated vision. Collectively then, what is possible with many Way-Showers demonstrating *the Way*?

When we each commit to happiness in every outcome and in all relationships – on a joyful journey in life we embark.

In this, we demonstrate we are free from conflict and have completed the curriculum. This neutrality cannot be faked, and we are born again as Way-Showers.

Seeing with mastery, we recognize our true occupation and are grateful to realize our part in God's plan. We see the perfection of highest outcomes and dedicate our lives to assist and counsel with presence, rather than authority.

In our demonstration, we are praising God for everything. Our thoughts, words and deeds are now of God's direction. We are no longer bound by false definitions of God.

Our Destiny

69 is the way of the Ancients; slow and simple. In slowness, there is an acceleration of wholeness. In simplicity, there is value.

We see how what we value draws our attention, and our how our attention focuses the energy of creation and to what effect. In this presence, we become truly connected with our purpose. The results are clear. It is essential we each live the values of the Ancients to realize how important we are to the whole.

The Ancient Ones

The Ancient Ones followed whispers of the heart
and built enlightened society,
while the rest of the world played musical chairs.

And then, when the music stopped,
the game was done, and all had lost - but one,
the Ancient Ones welcomed everyone home.

NowHere

Our immediate destiny is set. There are no alternate routes. Our assignment is to love what is, enjoy the ride and look upon all with Master's Eyes to envision the compassionate reality. The true reality. The natural and authentic existence we hid from ourselves. The reality that exists just beyond the river's bend.

The more that join this joyful journey, the more impact upon the collective. *All I must do is be in the Stream.* It takes far less effort together to be in the Stream. We are glad we co-create our destiny through collective vision. We can jump in, enjoy the ride, and invite everyone. *There is nothing to fear.*

It's therefore essential to go where our heart wants us to be. There are no obligations in Single Stream, but following the heart keeps us in the most efficient flow.

There is always a way, a ticket and a bed for those who are meant to be anywhere. No one sacrifices anything. Everything is provided and already done. It couldn't be any different.

Unless we allow our doubts room to surface.

Oftentimes familiarity creates a false sense of belonging. We imagine the maze as just good enough to tolerate our confusion, reflecting our belief in honorable sacrifice.

Vacating the maze then, is rattling to our false sense of stability. Like turbulence, we are disoriented exiting the atmosphere of a separated consciousness. Sometimes in our confusion, we try and go backward.

We fear we will lose ourselves.

"Who am I?

What will become of me?

True Vision is to Realize:

*The only sacrifice,
is of the thought of sacrifice itself.
To leave sacrifice and arrive home without it,
is of no sacrifice at all.*

We must then, be certain: *It can only be good to live without conflicting thoughts.* No one can lose anything of truth or of value, for without conflict there can be no sacrifice.

The choice to be happy no matter what, removes all conflict. Happy people are not in conflict. Separated thoughts do not lead to happiness. How could they? Separated thoughts then, are an investment in unfulfilled promises. The choice to be happy regardless, thus overrides all agreements of conflict. The false cannot be true.

For a spell, we might have to choose happiness every hour, or perhaps every moment. It does not matter. How many times we choose to see with Master's Eyes is irrelevant. We keep choosing until we don't have to choose. We keep choosing until we are certain. *There is no wiggle room in certainty.*

Now committed, we are released from what we required escaping, and the demonstration begins.

*Hold the Vision and Trust the Process
Where we are going is perfectly perfect.
The Way is through the Master's Eyes.*

It is Already Done

Chapter VI
The Bridge

Somewhere along the process of awakening, each of us realizes that giving and receiving are one and the same. We extend as directed by our intuition and are rewarded in ways we couldn't have imagined.

We see how focusing on 'getting' first is an imbalance of natural law.

Our corrected vision sees the truth of intertwining light and dark becoming one in compassionate manifestation. Way-Showers are the material demonstration then, of *Making Light of the Dark*. We are better for it. And glad for it. Life can only get brighter from here.

Way-Showers cannot tell anyone what to change. Yet anyone can change by desiring an awakening of the heart. Likewise, this book can only prescribe suggestions on how to initiate change. Simply get into the spirit of these words and discover the aliveness of the message for you. Your heart already knows.

We are already in communication with God, the Ascended Masters and the Angelic Realm. Christ is of all hearts. Simply choose to be happy and feel, *I am already in the Stream. Everything happens exactly in right timing for advancement.*

Oh, and another thing…

Have you ever missed an exit, or a turn in the road, had the wrong directions, or simply didn't know exactly where you were going?

Let's put you in a canoe going down a lazy little river on a pleasant afternoon.

Can you imagine this? Seeing the grassy banks, the trees reaching out and the quiet sounds of the water kissing the rocks along the shoreline as you float gently down the stream, dragging the paddle as steerage.

So peaceful it is, you can close your eyes and simply drift along with the current. Even if you nodded off, you would simply bump softly into the shoreline.

The kiss of warmth from the sun on your cheeks and the gurgling sound of the water causes a deep relaxation. A momentary snooze.

Awakening, you notice the river is moving slightly faster now, and you become more alert to your surroundings. Keeping the canoe pointed forward, a bend in the river comes into view, as the current picks up still. There are more rocks on the shore than before, and the terrain is steeper.

Approaching the turn, the river is beginning to lightly churn. Ahead there is white noise. A waterfall.

Intrigue and a slight twinge move through your abdomen.

Around the bend, the river expands, shallows and spreads into a large fan of water. There are rocks in the water now. The relief of the banks is steeper again, providing a magnificent display of beauty, light and sound.

The scene is breathtaking and beckons to be explored. The water is still navigable and there is plenty of room to maneuver. It sounds like a big waterfall. You can hear it pounding below and feel its energy. The spray of the churning water is misting upward into the valley and obscuring the view.

How close to the edge can you get and not get swept over the waterfalls themselves? Is there is a way to gain a glimpse of what is beyond by going a bit further? Is there a passage through? How are you going to continue?

The only way is to go further into the mist.

You already know as you advance toward the falls, you will begin to expend more energy paddling against the quickening current - and at some point, you don't know exactly, a combination of bravado, fatigue, agility, foolishness and false determination causes you cross to an invisible line – *the point of no return* - and be swept into the falls.

The Point of No Return

Our addictions are seeded quietly with lazy river thoughts that lull us into a trap. It doesn't seem like much at first, so we take a little trip.

We become enamored coming closer to the waterfall. There is excitement as we get suddenly pulled into something we were not going to do. Lines blur, we get lost and stumble.

We seem to like this game because we keep coming back. There's an extraordinary thrill to it. We are convinced we can stay on this side of the point of no return even though our experience has clearly shown we succumb to the waterfall repeatedly.

Usually, we wake up saying something like, "I feel terrible." We just expended a lot of energy on something that does not feel good. We don't feel good about what we did or what was said. We don't feel good about any of it, so we say, "I'm sorry," and promise to steer clear in the future. "But wow, what a trip. Remember how much 'fun' we had? Yeah."

Now we have set a boundary: It could be anything. "I won't gossip anymore, or play politics, or drink, lie, overeat, gamble, criticize, ghost, argue, date (wo)men like that, engage in casual sex, flirt, overspend, get high, fight or zone out with media."

By setting a boundary, it means we have judgement and are trying to control the situation. We have labeled someone or something as dangerous or bad and we are attempting to bar them from affecting us.

By doing so we affirm a false thought system with additional separated thoughts. Our human vision is reporting a danger, and we are reacting with justification and overthinking.

For example, when we use labels (narcissist,) we block others from growth with our human eyes, which reflects darkness we cannot perceive. We place a fixed image of the label in our minds, like a photograph. With this boundary, we invest in the problem with our creative sight, our will.

With human eyes, we fail to realize we created the distortion, and judgment is of the perceiver, not the perceived. Then our maze offers again, the same conflict disguised as something else, which we engage with similar effect.

Our labels and boundaries then, reveal the blocks in our sight. To remove the block, we must do something different, something new.

In most modern psychology, religion and addiction behavioral programs, we attempt to wall off people or circumstance to prevent addiction. We fail to see, *boundaries feed addiction*.

Utilizing everything from self-help, better friends, new hobbies and routines, we mostly practice fear and avoidance – to **not go with** the river.

We must see this.

Our path is predetermined.
The waterfall is unavoidable.
The journey to the waterfall is correct because it's the only one.
Our way out is through, *Eyes of the Master*.

Human memory and our environment report to us once we go past the point of no return, we're going over. We see no other possibility, which creates no other options. We have labeled the situation and placed a fixed outcome in our minds.

What is truly before us, however, is something vastly different than what we are conditioned to see. Our maze of thought creates the appearances of choice points in the river, but in truth, there are none.

Therefore, we will, to see something new, something real. We can pause, breathe and investigate to observe.

> *The Wise Slow Down*
> *When the World Speeds Up*

Our opportunity to explore the gap is hiding in plain sight. To discover a new route, we must change our bond with time.

We've all had the experience of having fun. "Where did the time go? I can't believe it happened so fast."

Time is pliable based on how we're feeling. When we are heavy with emotion, time goes by slow, and when we're light and free, it might go by fast, or we become incredibly efficient. And sometimes, we don't recall how we got from one place to another, as if we leaped forward somehow.

One moment we are in conversation, the next in a fight. One day our lover is our friend, and that evening our opponent. One minute we are sober, and then we've lost chunks of time and our life. One moment we are in peace, and the next in conflict.

How *did* we go from the lazy river to over the falls again?

In the background, our separated thoughts silently built a case for justified reactions – as a reflection of the eroding boundaries we set. What was a commitment, became but a hurdle. Then our lazy river got upset, and **in a flash,** we were over the falls and into a familiar (reactive) situation again.

It's the 'gap in a flash' that conceals our destiny.

The Gap in the Flash

The gap in the flash is a gateway to an expansion of awareness. Our separated thoughts fractured our vision, so we see something that is not there. We experience a gap. We skip from one experience to another quickly down a well-worn invisible path. Now we feel regret.

A question might be: *How is the lesson my soul wants me to learn and the thing I am avoiding, the same?*

The answer is in the gap. The gap is covered by shame and guilt swept under the rug or out of view. All our hidden hurts we don't like to acknowledge. We do not look, and therefore we do not see. We skip right over. By skipping ahead, we validate the past and make it real – and we ensure a return trip.

Outside the gap, our attempts to manage characters and behavior is non-effective and only leads to more conflict. We have learned this through repeated error. Whatever is in the gap then, we must investigate and explore to find our way out of the maze. God must be in the gap. It pulls at us for a reason.

We can say: *Perhaps this is a call for love from my soul to love the reflections I see.*

A Call for Love

In truth, we recreate experiences to position ourselves to finally answer the call, yet we can only answer the call when we do not react. Rushing ahead to the solution will not work. We have learned this lesson too. We cannot rush the gap, nor God. Both are already within. *We already have for what we search.*

The gap though, is covered by a multitude of secretive micro-mini judgements that instantly build a case against all challengers, so our emotional undergarments are not exposed.

To explore the gap, a spiritual warrior must be born in us. By this point of spiritual awakening, we have tried almost everything but going into the gap with reverence and humility. Only a compassionate heart can truly explore the gap.

We know the Grail is here, and we have been preparing by mastering the art of non-resistance in the face of testing. And testing most assuredly comes in the gap. We have set the stage for transformation; in us and them. We are certain for a happy outcome, for we know if we are not - we will not get one.

We also know reacting makes the false real, and initiates conflict. *Conflict always takes us over the waterfall.*

We also know, it is our ability to love which allows for the unmasking of the untrue, and the disarming of our illusionary opponent. With this certainty, we are neutral, unfazed and appear to be doing nothing, and in a sense we are.

Going into the gap, is to go beyond all red flags and reasoning to test our certainty in love. Determined to see no differences and be led by our intuition, we are guided to say and do the right things to collapse duality and bring unity to the situation.

Right and wrong, success and failure, rich and poor, black and white, red and blue, us and them, sickness and health, all become one in compassion, when we play our cards correctly.

A purification happens by engaging our challenges with love. In the moments of this suspended judgment, with the Master's Eyes, we can get free of past and future for an instant purification. We can release anger and confusion, glide past reactivity and gain a new relationship with time – simply by being neutral and authentic.

Gliding Past Reactivity

Now when we find ourselves in the lazy river, we can be more playful and curious. We can observe ourselves going into an addictive thought pattern, about anything: being right, sexual pursuits, thrill-seeking, spending, lying, overthinking, people pleasing, complaining, oversharing, manipulation or greed.

We can say to ourselves, *Okay, right, I have been here before.*

I have noticed an anomaly in this pattern of thinking. I can be aware and watch. By observing thoughts, I become neutral. In neutrality, all thoughts are rendered meaningless. Rather than believe them and react, I choose to see beyond.

In exploring the gap with observance, time becomes malleable in the suspension of judgement and control. Old choices fade, and a new doorway appears. What used to be invisible, is now suddenly there. The illusionary choices are not. Time is still.

We are peering through the Master's Eyes.

True Vision alchemizes lust, seduction, addiction and insanity into freedom. Our willingness to slow down and observe with love - our presence - allows us to slow down the scene: *I can remain on the edge – between succumbing and abstinence, maneuvering the canoe - allowing old thoughts to go over the waterfall, until True Vision reveals another route.*

Again, this is the melding point of dark and light in the Yin Yang, the dance of masculine and feminine, and the alchemy of refining base metal into gold. We are the heart of a labyrinth.

With our separated thoughts, we had blocked the exit from the maze. Disguised it well, we did.

Addiction is abstinence. Abstinence blocks the natural flow of energy of life, promoting rigidity and morality. Abstinence attempts to keep us from what we fear and is not real. When we stay away from the waterfall, we won't experience what is beyond, until the flood. Therefore, we remain in the maze.

Addiction is also succumbing. Succumbing is destructive, a detour and a dead end. A desecration to our temples. How long are we going to allow ourselves to feel good for the moment, while we live in regret? We are still in the maze.

Lesson of *the Way*

The lesson of *the Way*, no matter how you view it - Yin Yang, 69, or Single Stream - reveals: *The choice points I see in the maze of life do not exist.* In our realization of the lesson, a previously unseen doorway opens. We see one path.

Which way becomes the Way.

Single Stream Waterfall

It simply wasn't in our awareness before.

Paddling around this great fan of water, we now see faint strands of light moving together just above the water's surface toward something we cannot understand, like a wispy cloud.

Instinctively we know to row with the light. The stream of light is going directly into the mist concealing the falls. Our rational mind once thought danger, but at this moment, something new is happening in our heart. We trust the lightness could only lead somewhere new, someplace good.

Enthusiastically, we dig with our paddle to row with the light. The stream of light begins to affect the trajectory of our canoe, until no additional effort is required. We are amused that *what I feared, is not real*. Floating along in the stream of light, the expanse beyond the waterfall becomes visible from above, as the water crashes below. We are inexplicably held by the light and feel completely at ease.

We are riding in a river of light beyond the fall.

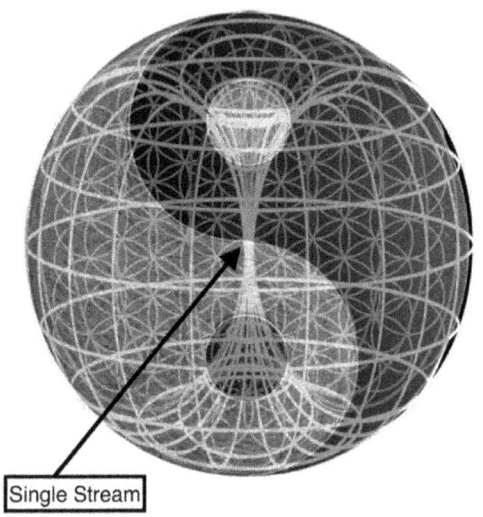

As we travel the river of light, we experience our multi-dimensionality. With True Vision, we find the labyrinth to be a blissful journey.

In the past we looked at a labyrinth on the ground with our human eyes. We couldn't see the spherical dimensions of space around it. We could only see a fraction of truth. The labyrinth and the Yin Yang we see on paper are but symbols of the inner dimensions of time and space orbiting us. We are as much of it, as it is of us.

All around us is a universe of energy flowing in perfection. We were so lost in the maze, we could not see our vastness as we do now. Now, we see the Single Stream as the center of our personal universe connects us to everything. Our inner guide is revealing our potential.

The Dowsing Rod

We all have a dowsing rod or an indicator. Call it intuition if you like. Its intelligence is infinite and leads us to fulfill our purpose. The dowsing rod is attuned to our Divine Blueprint. All we must do is listen to the whispers of our heart and follow inspiration. Along the way we learn and receive gifts that complement our purpose.

As we learn to listen, we are led beyond conflict into peace by way of *entrainment*.

Entrainment

Everything is alive and of the same substance. With the breath of God all have consciousness, and all fulfill purpose. Divine intelligence is boundless and reciprocal in all living things. All are vital tributaries of the Stream and naturally find their way.

We are all already functioning - no matter what we perceive - perfectly on our evolutionary track. We are learning how to use the inner guide to explore our aliveness with the things, people, situations, animals and activities that inspire loving life.

We are moving past Law of Attraction into the Law of Unfoldment, which is to say something new happens in terms of how we experience life. We thought we were doing life. Now we discover life is doing us.

Self-Organizing

Law of Attraction was our curriculum. Law of Unfoldment is our now demonstration. In surrender, the Blueprint reveals our perfect purpose in step with our evolving sight.

Our Divine Blueprint self-organizes everything required in the absence of our resistance. Our intuitive actions pay much greater dividends. As we become aligned with the truth of our being, a journey of least effort is initiated – home. Our determination for a joyful journey has led us from the maze:

I release my perception of a world that is insane or mad or at war to see an entirely different world. I join with those who see, in the True Reality. Together we will, a better existence for all.

In the Stream all play roles designed for themselves, an evolved version of their human-self, less the conflict. We advance our roles by tuning into our dowsing rods and following the heart. We naturally entrain with others on a similar journey. Rapid acceleration occurs in evolutionary flow.

The curriculum is now a demonstration. Way-Showers are naturally led into life situations where our ability to *Make Light of the Dark* becomes useful to the whole. Seeing the True Reality, we assist others in spiritual awakening through art, counsel, ministry and ceremony to discover peace within.

Earth is Calling. Who is Listening?

Single Stream picks us up, enlivens our spirit and cleanses our minds – by connecting us with infinite wisdom. It is time to embrace our destiny. It can only be better than we imagined. We will all celebrate co-creating a reality of peace, love and understanding. A world where everyone gets what they want.

It is vital to see, I am already getting what I want.
What I want equals how I spend my attention.
I always gain the yield of my attention.
I can easily refocus on true value.

We must become fiercely committed to our strength of mind. Our empowerment lies in how and where we aim our sight, and how un-distractable we can become in our art of non-resistance.

We can coach ourselves: *What I'm supposed to know, is exactly what I discover. What I require is always provided. How I am inspired by the heart reflects my true responsibility. I have exactly what I desire. And what I desire, is exactly what I have.*

I thought I had choices, and though I imagined I was lost, I see now I was always on my path. I realize, to believe anyone could have done differently, is to suffer. When I notice suffering, I immediately recognize I am in the wrong thought system. By accepting human perception as false, I refocus. "I don't want to see them, me, or this situation in this way any longer."

For instance, if we are in any relationship that appears to be toxic, we must take responsibility for the manifestation and change our mind immediately. We must initiate change from the only effective place – inside - using the desire we have cultivated in the heart to be happy and in the Stream.

Now we mean it when we say; My *perception of _____ must be of my creation, I no longer want to see _____ this way. I choose a happy outcome seeing with Master's Eyes. I replace my mental images with God's. Thy Will Be Done.*

Everyone has unique gap experiences, and none of them wrong. Everyone has the same purpose: To learn to love the lessons and characters in the gap. In the gap, there is a universe to explore of non-reactivity and personal responsiveness. In the gap, we discover the parts of us we hid from ourselves. In the gap, we learn to love everything we find.

Essentially, the game is:

Reacting is to go back to one.
Listening in presence advances two.

Both involve learning, and both are necessary.

We may have similar experiences repeatedly to fully expand our vision into truth. Looking for incremental progress rather than reasons for failure, helps us slow down and become more present. A deliberate focus on learning, accelerates growth.

We must be courageous to explore the gap repeatedly, in life and in meditation - until we have no reaction at all. No reaction is the reflection of the truth: *There is nothing there. There is nothing to forgive. I manufactured the conflict I experienced.*

Lesson of the Gap

There are no gaps in truth. When all is forgiven, I experience no gap. Purification removed the distortion. Nothing is now hidden. We see clearly how all conflict is created by human perception. Therefore, no justification for anger, confusion or impatience remains. We rediscover the peace we always have been.

Butterfly Effect

The utter simplicity of how neutral energy works gives humanity the capacity to become change. The quickest way to change, is to change our language. It's important to realize language is generated directly from thoughts.

Aligned with God's Thoughts, our language naturally becomes of the heart and no longer conflicted. We are not participating in (people pleasing) any longer. The withdrawal of the horizontal energy from (people pleasing) and into a vertical stream of energy without conflict, changes how people interact with us, and what experience is rendered.

This allows us to go beyond the well-worn storylines we have abused for eternity, *perpetrator and victim*. Once we see how one cannot exist without the other, we will cease to project the equivalent distortion by vacating separate thoughts. Now we can trust again. We do not require rescuing. We feel safe and honored. This is our choice and our only one voice.

Hearts aligned amplifies coherence.
Coherence is everyone's natural flow state.
In coherence, we remember who we are.
When I remember, I am aligned.

It is a Choiceless Choice.
I am glad choice is choiceless.
Only good happens when I feel good.
Being certain is my choice.

Part Three
The Solution

VII – *Down By the River - 73*
VIII – *Planting Seeds - 85*
IX – *MisCreation – 89*
X – *Connecting to Single Stream – 105*

Chapter VII
Down By the River

Thank you for joining me at the fire down by the river. One more indulgence before you go. This one is a bit more personal, just so you know.

After the pandemic began in Spring of 2020, I had a lucid dream. It was as real as the dream of life. With my two hands, I pulled out my eyeballs and was blinded. Intuitively, I dropped to the floor crawling on my hands and knees padding the carpet feeling for new eyes.

I came across what felt like peeled grapes. Cupping them in my hands, I pressed them into my eye sockets, stood and felt my way to the bathroom. In the reflection of the mirror, I saw only illuminated Master's Eyes, like on the cover of this book. All else was dark. In a rush of energy, I woke up. I knew I had seen change, and that was all.

Then the headaches began. Purification was underway.

I could never have imagined the sweeping changes. Everything I thought I valued stripped away as migraines daily dropped me to all fours. What seemed like suffering at the time, I now see as purification. What seems liked a series of unfortunate events and poor decisions, were merely the symptoms of a sweeping change of mind. A purging.

The initiation of the lucid dream was the beginning of mastering *the Way*. It was the beginning of the purification I had both wanted and avoided my entire life. It was essential. The only way out was through… and the only relief was to forgive.

I made and kept a promise every day - *I will not sleep with anger in my heart*. Sometimes that meant not sleeping at all.

There were no other choices. My response was as this book suggests. Day after day, I followed my heart and embraced the process, all the while holding a vision of inner peace and external expression. Two years later with nothing left, I became a nomad.

Being a nomad, essential to getting to know the fabric of humanity, took me through the Southeastern United States, Portland, Oregon and then to Mexico before returning to the United States to live in Crestone Colorado, Taos New Mexico, and now Sedona, Arizona.

Then on Valentine's Day 2025 just a few days after beginning to write this book, and nearly five years after the dream, the Eyes reappeared while in meditation. This time however, I saw from the Master's point of view.

I had forgotten the dream, yet it had not forgotten about me.

What I see now, is the same I saw before the headaches, only without conflict.

The journey is worth it.
We can't fight our way to peace.
Boundaries are delay tactics to love.
Separated thoughts are held by not feeling.
We will repeat the past until the past is forgiven.
Past hurts are the graven images we worship.
Feeling is the way to open the heart.
In the heart is a Single Stream.
In Single Stream, we can open the gap.
In the gap is potential, peace and satisfaction.
In the gap, is a pathway to the True Reality.
In the True Reality, there is no gap.
The journey is worth it.

Forgiveness

Forgiveness isn't letting people of the hook or righting a wrong. It is correction of vision.

Forgiveness is correctly seeing what happened in a separate thought system was seen with distorted perception. Therefore, we cannot be certain of what happened, or if it happened at all.

We are glad to be uncertain about what we thought was real with human eyes. This initiates the desire to change our mind.

The perfection of this and every outcome is to bring us back to our only choice, which is: *I choose what is already true.* There isn't any conflict now, nor has there never has been. We can rejoice. We can choose joy right here, right now and be free.

I am glad everything happened like it did to bring me to this moment: I can release all ideas of wrongdoing and enter a slipstream of energy that leads to Heaven on Earth. Now here. I can surrender and let go now, and it can be instant.

A Mass Forgiveness

It is impossible to forgive case by case. It requires too much effort. Plus, it is not necessary. Since everyone could only see wrongly in a separated thought system, all are pardoned.

In truth, *It is already done. I have forgiven, everyone.*

A Mass Forgiveness

I forgive everyone, for all of time.
For every angry look & petty crime.
For every bullet, bomb and war plane.
For every betrayal & crooked campaign.
For every dirty deed and every one's lies.
For every deception and all murder tries.
For every sexual deed, by sleight of hand.
I forgive all with love, so only love stands.
For none are guilty in using silly rhyme.
We forgave everyone, for all of time.

New Vision

To be happy in the human condition, despite the condition, is nearly impossible.

In a separated mind, the goal is not happiness – even though it may appear that way. It is tolerance and survival through conflict. We are addicted to feeling terrible. So addicted, we reach for the same poison day after day. To be truly happy therefore requires a letting go of the way we were taught, so our original system can operate in the way of its natural design.

To be in Single Stream is to be in the flow. It is always the right moment, right time, right place, right people, right situations. There is no arguing with or judging the flow. It simply **is,** and **it is always** flowing perfectly, regardless of our perception.

We are not trying to control flow, trying to fix flow or give flow suggestions on how to improve. We are simply present and responsive in ways feeling right in the heart. *This is our model for life, with ourselves – and with others.* *

(Read this paragraph twice.) *

To be in Single Stream is to use simple loving language. Solution-oriented language about possibility, potential, miracles and creativity, or "Linguistic Intelligence." *I have lost interest in language that divides, labels, judges or criticizes.*

We must see, our conflicting thoughts send ripples of static into our awareness altering our perception of flow. In our seeing, we can make immediate correction simply by noticing anomaly - then shifting our gaze to what is truly real and valuable.

The problems of the world cannot be solved in the world. The separated world is by design entropic and exclusionary. Our only *choice*… our only *chance* then, is to release our density and forgive. Then, and only then, are we light enough to float above and travel beyond the waterfall.

Only in total forgiveness can we see what the Master sees.

By focusing on, or fixing problems, we worsen the problem.
By forgiving the world en masse, we advance in the solution.
By placing our attention on what is valuable we enable vision.
By withdrawing our attention from conflict, we are prepared.

Prepared for... *Well, What is Next?*

There's a lot of chatter about ascension, aliens, conspiracy, Earth splitting into New Earth, war, Revelations, cataclysms and a second coming.

It is like a pick your adventure and choose your ending novel – except this one is true. Whatever is believed becomes true for the believer. Perhaps this line is worth repeating: *Whatever is believed, becomes true for the believer.*

There is nothing to fear however, for with the Master's Eyes of exemplary compassion we see clearly: Beyond all human beliefs: *All streams flow into God's Single Stream.*

What a load off... *It doesn't matter.* We can allow everyone to be in their experience, knowing their experience can only guide them home. Regardless of what anyone experiences, it is temporary before they return to God. *All paths lead home.*

It feels good, to release worries. I wish everyone the best and let them be free. Including those who are in our lives.

Releasing worry is vital as it appears the number of possibilities for our future is diminishing. It looks we have gone past several exits and find ourselves on an unmapped highway without any rest stops in sight. It seems like we are low on fuel.

Our eyes are burning. We are tired.

There is a waterfall ahead. We sense it. A watershed moment. We cannot see what approaches beyond the horizon - a something - we cannot fathom. No human forecast could possibly model or measure this potential or get it right.

Something amazing is happening ahead - an opportunity to be something new. We won't be able to comprehend or to see it clearly beforehand. If we are open, peaceful and enthusiastic, we are aligned. If we are in fear, we can realign.

All we can do is prepare.
We are empowered in preparation.
We are glad, knowing it can only be good.
In not knowing we have faith and enjoy the ride.
As Way-Showers, we demonstrate One life.
We are glad to lead the Way for others.
Where all streams become One.

The Straw that Almost Breaks the Camel's back

We don't know how much longer we can tolerate the burden. We are carrying too much weight and are unbalanced.

Now, we realize the seduction.
We tossed the fuel *and* lit the fuse.
And then we blamed others for our ruse.
So, bring your gas cans and your lighters too,
We're going to celebrate and party with you.

Compassionate Economy

Our human view of success is the poison we consume each day.

Rather than looking out for the whole, we engage our best interests as we see them. Were we to see our interests with True Vision, we would instantly recognize that giving and receiving are the same, *and* that it is impossible to sacrifice this truth.

The quotient for success then, isn't about how much _____ we have. The true quotient of success is: *How much can I give with what I have?*

Why would anyone interrupt the flow of the Stream that is always giving? Why would anyone hold on, to what is infinite?

Answer: Unworthiness. (Wrong thought system.)

Our current geo-political social economic systems reflect a collective thought of unworthiness. Changing anything in the system is a fruitless endeavor, because without a change in collective thinking, what we wish to change is only reinforced.

The same is true for anyone. What we wish to change is only reinforced when we focus on symptoms, rather than root cause.

Our separated thinking is the root cause of all conflict in our personal universe. When we realize this, we are empowered to change our thoughts, and our world. Everyone in our Universe then must shift with us in the absence of conflict. *What I gaze upon with love flourishes. What I withdraw from diminishes.*

There is a yearning to be free and a willingness to feel encouraged as we sit here on the bank of the river. Maybe we don't need to start any more fires.

You might ask:

Is it possible all my thoughts affect all others?

By thinking with God's Thoughts, would possibilities emerge I never considered?

By giving up ideas of scarcity, will I discover true satisfaction?

What does humanity desire and need, I could offer with passion?

How can I be in Single Stream consistently?

For the final scenes of our play, we can each make a simple shift. By upgrading our definition of <u>success</u> to *compassion*, we shift our focus from <u>getting</u> and investigate devotion to a cause. In doing so, we accelerate into the gap.

Our society would be greatly assisted by the simplification. Our hearts would be greatly empowered with this devotion. The new definition of success, therefore, is reduced to simply one word: *Compassion*.

Compassion

Everyone is successful with their participation.

What would happen if everyone began helping everyone?

What would happen, if compassion became a fashion?

Ready to embark upon a journey of True Vision?

Ask and Ye Shall Receive, For

It is Already Done.

Chapter VIII
Planting Seeds

It looks like one river flowing by, from where we sit by the fire.

Zooming out, we see that our little river is part of a vast intricate network of life energy, circulating all waters on Earth in unison. Were we to throw anything into the moving water, we would be in truth be affecting the entire network. Throwing unconsciously, pollutes. Offering consciously, heals.

In our heart, is the bank of Single Stream. It looks like one river. Our individual river. Zooming out we see it as a part of vast intricate network of life energy connecting all to One, circulating thought and feeling through all vortices, always giving birth to new creations.

As we sit with the river, we realize we each are the center of an infinite labyrinth of connected living waters of light. With each thought, we impact the entire system. Everyone. Everything. What is our focus, what is our game?

What thoughts and with what intent are you throwing into y(our) river? Are you polluting the living waters, or are you seeding a compassionate reality? Is it about you, focused on getting? Is it worry, comparison, shame or fear? Are they your thoughts, God's thoughts or someone else's? What are you responsible for putting into humanity's living waters?

I spent much of my life trying to fit into the colonial arena of success. However, it turns out I was too pure to get lost in the game. It appears I lost, but I am merely symptomatic of the lesson of my Divine Blueprint. We all must learn to let go.

Funny thing is, I was always perfectly on my path, I only kept trying to fit into the wrong system. My thoughts about life and myself were not in truth. Does this ring true for you?

In Single Stream, I am reconditioned to not know. When I don't know, life becomes an enjoyable dance of intuition, action, response and impact. I become free of expectation, sabotage and missing out when I choose to be happy regardless in my expression. My judgments fade. I can give and receive freely.

We are all going to lose everything, that is certain. None of it belongs to us, anyhow. Once we realize everything is God's, we can refocus on generosity and lighten our loads for the coming change. It is not valuable where we are going anyway.

Who would mis-manage God's resources at a time like this? What then could God's resources be best used for?

I would focus on that.

Chapter IX
MisCreation

Why not accept our true inheritance in the releasing of illusion?

We must then, go right to the edge and not succumb to our disease, nor ignore the power of the falls. We have long been seduced by cheap thrills and swept over, and equally seduced by withholding our voice in fear of the fall.

Our disease? *We Exploit Creation*

Exploitation of Creation

We have suppressed the feminine by overusing the masculine energy to control, lust, conquer, legislate and profit. We have made laws, imprisoned people, and built walls. Yet the feminine in all of us does not feel safe.

Our environment is for profit and our education hijacked; we are challenged by our collective disregard for the natural. Our media is seductive and to that we have given our will. We have become the commercial television programming.

We are all connected to a vast intricate system of polluted human vision. Contaminated with distorted images of miscreation – fueled by a collective unwillingness to forgive.

Upon further observation, we see it more clearly:

The whole play is plainly ordinary – lacking any true creativity. It's quite unfulfilling and hasn't any genuine substance at all.

Isn't it obvious?

What we do with sexual vitality is how we treat Creation.
How we view, sell and have sex, is our secret sedation.
We sacrifice our integrity for somebody else's say.
Generally, we skip past and look another way.
We tolerate societal glorification of desire.
All are drunk and going even higher.

Is this not an illusionary world? How funny, and what an extraordinary paradox. It was the orgasm that gave us this life!

The disease of our addiction is skipping past the gap to get the immediate reward. We treat (*sex & everything*) like a conquest rather than an experience of God.

We have lost the sacredness for the very act of love that gave us life, for Creation itself. We go for the (orgasm) like it's the prize, rather than realizing lovemaking is a sacred intercession and intertwining of the dark and light powers of creation.

To find the conflict we have with ourselves, we must not look any further than how we feel about sexuality.

No wonder we like war. Our conflicts in the world are but mirror images of how conflicted we are about how we wield the power of creation. Our underground thoughts, feelings and indulgences are not isolated to our little river. The energy we connect with flows into and from all our relationships, transactions, partnerships and expressions.

We are seduced by the darkness of sexuality, rather than in alignment with the light. Our focus is the body. On looks and perceived needs, validating lust, greed and status. It is difficult to recognize this from inside our separated world, with separated thoughts – except we feel neither satisfied nor happy.

Satisfied happy people treat living beings well. Those in separated thoughts do not.

We actually think, no one else knows "what I am dealing with." We actually think keeping secrets protects us. We actually think poor me stories are true. We actually think we are justified in our miscreation, while others are not. And, we actually think we can solve our problems with walls and war.

We must think then, we have two worlds - the world of our thoughts, and the world of God. Yet, they are the same. One is 96, and the other 69. One is a microclimate, while the other is a universe. One is a grain of sand, while the other is all sand on all beaches. One is a drop of water, while the other is the ocean. We are making a big deal with separated thoughts about what is nothing at all. We have blinded ourselves with complexity. This is the illusion.

Imagine for a Moment

What if, the way we made love and lived life became a glorification of God? Now, there can be no more conflict.

Opening the *gap in the flash*, we recognize that miscreation will never lead us to God, nor will lust. We discover how nearly everything in which we have participated has been colored by our conflict with sexuality. We also discover nothing we engage on the horizontal plane will ever yield true satisfaction when we treat it like a conquest.

And we are glad for this realization. We are becoming enlightened to our authentic power.

The Horizonal Plane

The horizonal plane is the conditional realm, or the maze. It is how we use thoughts, language and action to get what *we think we want*. A simplistic example would be the exchange of money for a product. Another would be: "If _____ (loves) me, then I will be (happy,) or even, "People are _____."

We look to the horizontal plane for everything, justice, satisfaction, approval, security, healing, validation, even revenge. With our separated thoughts hiding the gap, we are in effect creating a looping effect confusing the order of creation. Rather than going to God for what we already have, we influence our environment to get what we think we want. Yet our thoughts are based in conflict, and mostly hidden.

Generally then, rather than validating truth by feeling our heart, we make something (or someone) wrong, not seeing the ridiculousness of our choice for more conflict. We are blind.

On the horizontal plane we are isolated from God. All thoughts, words and deeds are **cause** in a closed system. Our experience is **effect**. Therefore, everything we create must have a condition attached, and it returns to us in a loop, usually dramatically.

Peace, love, abundance and happiness have no conditions for they are both the cause and effect of God. Any tactic we use to feel better or solve a problem, is trying to fill a non-existent hole. We are trying to solve the equation of a closed false system. The only solution is to vacate the system.

Simply by being honest we reconnect with our sovereignty; *Wow, for the most part everything I have done, thought, and said has been in reference to what I see happening on the horizontal plane. I can see how this puts me into conflict, because that is the nature of being on the horizontal plane. I am not interested in these conditions any longer.*

With this awareness, we can see. *Wow, I notice I am having thoughts like 'if something or someone would do or be different, or approve of me, <u>then</u> I would be happy.' This cannot be true. I release these thoughts into the Stream to be purified.*

When we do not feel good or become stuck in drama, we have turned off our dowsing rod. We make decisions based on intellect, reasoning, and experience (what's covering the gap.)

Without a dowsing rod, we have stripped ourselves of power. The dowsing rod represents far more than an antenna, or some kind of navigational device. It is the mechanism in which to forge a relationship with God, establishing faith and certainty. We forge certainty through listening and following guidance. When what we intuit matches our experience, we develop trust. In trust, anything is possible.

All is Provided For Now

In Single Stream, there are no conditions to receiving, and this is why our mantra for New Earth is: *All is Provided For Now*.

When our energy is apart from the horizontal plane, and into vertical alignment, we become everything without condition. What we require is given to us because we are present with creation. *We are able to receive our divine inheritance.*

Our demonstration has nothing to do with anything worldly. It doesn't matter how we arrive at this awareness, through a church or synagogue, or perhaps by way of metaphysics or paganism. It could arrive by lightning bolt, or imprisonment. None of it matters. It doesn't matter what your parents believed, or what society believes. It doesn't matter what your friends believe. To be concerned of opinion, including our own, or to take anything personal is living on the horizontal plane. Aren't we all exhausted from this approach?

Going Vertical

Each of us then, has a simple responsibility to go vertical with our energy: Rise above and become impervious to conflict – like when opposite magnets cannot touch.

All addiction, illness and relationship dynamics happen on the horizontal plane in drama loops. Going vertical relieves us of the conditional reality of our symptoms of separate thoughts.

The simple solution to our seemingly complex problem is to go vertical. Going vertical is the only prayer we will ever need. It sees the solution. *God is everything, and is doing everything.*

Going vertical is giving everything to God and then riding the vision of your life, in joy.

The transition is simple. The instant we recognize a thought on the horizontal plane, like "I want them, or life, to be different," we can pause and give those thoughts an opportunity to go over the waterfall, while we ride the edge. We can vertically align and invite God into our hearts. We can do nothing.

The effort is minimal. However, persistence is vital. From the lips of the guru with whom I studied for seven years; "Training the mind, is like training a puppy on a leash. When the puppy is pulling in a different direction, you lightly pull on the leash. Eventually, the puppy learns."

Strength of mind is the ability to release a separated thought instantly. We learn to refocus on the now. And in this mastery, we become free. No one can do it for us, yet in acceptance of responsibility, we receive the assistance we require. *Now, all things of miscreation diminish from my sight.*

What this means for you: What is falling away or apart, is being 'taken' because of an energy shift. Loss is not personal. Loss is a symptom of realignment. Therefore, what is next must be aligned with God and worth your patience. It must be good!

Therefore, in any relationship with an employer, lover, friend or property that ends or is in process of ending, the best thing to do is bow out with gratitude and generosity, as a demonstration of the mantra for New Earth:

All is Provided for Now.

Knowing what is meant for you is already given in the absence of conflict, makes it easier to let go in style. You can leave every situation better than you found it, including you – thereby setting the stage for beautiful manifestation.

I have seen through the Master's Eyes. It is obvious now. I can take a break from distraction. I can rest. I can accept. I can feel. I can forgive. I can grieve and release. I can communicate openly. I can reconnect with the sacredness of sensuality. I can experience true intimacy, and I will these to be my experience.

In my withdrawal from a world of separated thoughts, a new world is given to me to experience. I am certain of this!

We can trust:

> *Lust for fame, money, greed and sex all fall apart –*
> *By bringing our awareness to the heart.*

We see humanity's zero-sum game. Yet we play on as if to insult our intelligence. We don't feel safe in a land of conquest. We don't feel abundant in a society of greed. We don't feel heard in the courts of justice. Our collective denial is restless. Our attempts at self-preservation have pushed us to the brink. Our solutions have only created more problems.

We must change then, by being willing to be changed.

Willingness to be Changed

If an entire thought system is but a tiny grain of sand on an infinite beach, then how difficult is it to change? Is it difficult, or hard? Perhaps it is simply *heart*.

We have read twice now, that losing sacrifice could not be much of a sacrifice. In truth, in the demonstration of our willingness, there is only one path out of the maze.

>Sacrifice,
>Sacrifice.

Our human thought system believes in "hard," rather than *heart*. Therefore, we must remove the hard shield covering the gap in our awareness.

To feel what is in the heart, we must sacrifice the hard. Then we will be able to see. It seems obvious, no?

In learning giving and receiving are one, the invitation to join Single Stream is extended by paradox.

>*By sacrificing sacrifice, I sacrifice nothing at all.*
>*Why then, is giving up nothing, so hard?*

Accepting ourselves and our life journey as a perfect learning device to deliver us to perfect love, makes our manifestation of our goal to be happy, easier.

We all know exactly what we do to fragment our attention. We know what it feels like to martyr our integrity. We know our games. We just don't know how to stop skipping, past the gap.

The very nature of Single Stream is always giving. It is always flowing, and always pure. The way to enter the Stream is by being neutral and doing nothing – which to the human viewpoint, has no value at all. Doing nothing and being neutral are the antithesis of human success standards and essential to becoming empowered as a life artist, or Way-Shower.

Simply being and doing nothing are the mechanisms giving birth to the desires of the heart, which have always been here – only shielded from view. Now we know where to place our attention, and we are excited for what is to be created.

Otherwise, we are too full. We literally have no room for God because we are too busy playing the roles of thinker and doer – rather than focused on being the finished product.

One Simple Action

By taking a few moments to imagine with feeling, a life of satisfaction, you are making room for God's finished product.

Forget about details and what you think you want – reach deep for the feeling of satisfaction beyond human thought. A little at a time, begin to cultivate a deep inner yearning to *love no matter what*. This one simple repeated action will allow Single

Stream to begin taking you beyond reactivity into the True Reality. This is the decision to be happy. And in this simple choice, God will meet you there.

We can learn to be still and feel: *By spending time in Single Stream, I am naturally purified. It doesn't have to be hard. It can be heart. Yes, Life is Heart. All I must do is be willing to be still and feel. This sounds perfectly perfect to me.*

We Already Know

We already know, the best thing any one (man) can do for humanity is to unplug from all forms of body worship, pornography, flirtatious chatter, pay for sex, fantasy, conquest and secret activities, to listen to the heart.

This would refocus his sexual energy into the heart for compassion, rather than to fragment the power of creation with myopic desire for a quick fix, or advantageous outcome. He would be less interested in war games of all kinds and lay aside fruitless competition and illusionary control tactics.

We already know, the best thing that any one (woman) can do for humanity is to use her voice and be patient with love. In honoring her sacred temple by wisely planting seeds, she becomes the womb of creation.

No longer a depository or silent partner in miscreation and degradation, she lays aside fruitless vanity and is nourished.

We already know, the best thing for all else, and everyone too:

> No matter what we think, let no more shame accrue.
> Get outside and enjoy nature to refresh the view.
> True intimacy is the way to break through.
> Be Simple and Be Like You.

All these changes are made for us, when we decide to sit in the Stream. The habitual patterns keeping us on the gerbil wheel are washed away with the tiny little effort of surrender. This answers our paradox of sacrificing sacrifice by being squarely in the middle of the labyrinth, our heart center.

> *I need do nothing.*
> *Forgiveness requires no sacrifice*
> *but of sacrifice itself.*

No matter what is in our rearview mirror, none of it matters in our choice. Nothing changes in acceptance, yet everything is made new. We remain the same people and enjoy life.

It's worth it to be alive. It's worth it to be healthy. It's worth it to learn to use our voice. It's worth it to learn to listen. It's worth it to slow down and live the Ancient Way. It's worth it to be dedicated to service. It's worth it, for God is the true measure of worth, and cannot be sacrificed. I am worthy of God's plan.

In the gap, we remember the purpose of every relationship.

The Purpose of <u>Every</u> Relationship is to Heal

Our purpose is to become whole. Human vision competes with healing, like a game of hide and go seek, rather than going straight for the solution. We avoid or indulge the shame, rather than sitting still with the illusion of shame.

When we recognize our (sexual) horizontal wants are revealing what we need to heal, rather than as a vehicle of temporary satisfaction for our uneasiness, we see a new path. We advance in the absence of conflict.

Our sexual cravings reflect both separated thoughts, and an avenue to wholeness. Bringing sexual longings to the heart rather than rushing forward into them, allows us to remember the gap. Here we explore how intuition and creativity blend to be the perfect vehicle for *Making Light of the Dark*.

The simplicity and power of vulnerability also releases us from the maze. We open the gap in transparent communication with our fellow brothers and sisters in Single Stream.

Our results are astonishing. In healing we receive everything.

Transparent communication without reactivity is a symptom of vacating the false thought system. So is integrity, abundance, health, enthusiasm and satisfaction. By seeing perfection in all, intimacy opens our cells of self-imprisonment. Boundaries dissolve and peace remains.

We discover changing our energetic structure is the way to end every difficult situation. We simply go vertical, by rising above.

Remember, aligning with Single Stream is to use heart's desire. When we desire something amazing, we are willing to practice the becoming, until we become the desire itself.

Be happy. Happiness does it all!

Here is the most exciting part:

An enlightened society builds itself when we let God work through our eyes, hands, ears tongues and heart. We're imagining what we must do to fix our world, is hard - when in truth, it is much simpler. It is simply (he)art. The divine balance between masculine and feminine. The art of love.

In our love, we see that New Earth is already here, and she is materializing through our collective seeing, through the Master's Eyes.

Come then. Jump into the Stream. Release your old ideas with joy, for it can only be good. Where we are going is perfectly perfect.

All is Provided for Now.

Chapter X
Connecting to Single Stream

When we notice we are not happy, confused or simply over thinking, we can pause and utilize the visualization of the waterfall's edge.

Allowing separated thoughts to go over the falls, we remain present to our environment regardless of the noise. *Any thoughts I cannot let go, I offer to the Stream.*

All creation is fluid, and the possibilities are endless from here. It comes down to our willingness to be purified, so choiceless choices emerge. *How willing am I, to be still and feel?*

As you feel, allow emotions to go over the falls. Everything bothersome, offer to the Stream with love and notice the change. God's living waters purify like pouring clean water into a dirty glass. Turbulence signals a churning of debris at the bottom, advancing us, despite a passing discomfort. Pouring fresh water in consistently, purifies the water.

I release all separated thoughts. I allow them to flow over and beyond. As I'm sitting amid the flood, my awareness opens, and I experience light flowing vertically through me. The space around me expands. I breathe with my heart in the acceptance of all and feel the energy lift my spirits.

Now, I allow the blessing of my memory to advance images of an unforgiven past, like frames of a movie. I appreciate and offer these images to the Stream. I am willing to be here in recognition of my thirst for joy, knowing there is nothing to fear in facing illusion. God or the Stream whatever you are - more than anything, I desire happiness. I want to be free in my expression, rather than to judge this beautiful mess anymore.

Somewhere about right now the tears start falling.

We are what we desire. All we must do is acknowledge our natural and true alignment to open a door to a new world. By being willing to know and feel God's love, we become peace.

Be courageous in the cultivation of a unique relationship with the Stream. You can tell it anything, and it will give you everything. There is nothing you "have to" do, be, or follow. Simply be agreeable. Your intuition guides perfectly.

In True Vision, we would not abandon anyone during a call for love – even ourselves. We therefore begin to enjoy the process.

If we are reactive, we are not in the Stream. Recognizing this, we can offer all anger to the Stream for transmutation with joy.

When we feel off, we can say: *I don't feel good. I must be in the wrong thought system. This approach is exhausting. I will slow down and feel my heart, to recognize illusion, and align with what is true. What can I feel to make room for joy? How can I answer my call for love?*

When we are certain in our communion with the Stream, we activate responsiveness and receive direction and answers. Our eyes are opened.

And, because it is fun, we can be ridiculously thankful: *I am grateful for everything that happened to bring me back to my one choice: To love no matter what.*

And, because we love creating, we can say and visualize with feeling: *Wouldn't be nice to experience _____?* For any request we make in neutrality, we know we receive the twin of our desire. In perfect creation then, who wouldn't be happy? We rejoice in the Stream with God, knowing *all is provided.*

We can boil everything then, down to one experiential lesson: *Authentic Action is Intuitive and can only lead to wholeness. Wholeness is born of least effort, or simply intuitive action.*

In True Reality, dimensions are different. What looks like miles of space with human eyes is merely the fabric of consciousness itself, malleable according to sight. What looked hard is not. What seemed impossible becomes *the Way*.

In Single Stream, anything is possible as we release our human ideas and boldly follow our heart. Our relationship with time and space is therefore modified as we become aligned with natural law and universal intelligence. We are rejuvenated in all areas of life, in harmony of equal exchange.

In our neutrality, we are certain. Certainty is empowerment as we demonstrate creating with 1% of the exertion we are accustomed. The results far exceed our previous efforts.

It turns out simplicity's yield, is abundance for all.

We might say:

I thought there were many rivers.
I thought they were many dreams,
Now I am wise enough, to see but a Single Stream.
Single Stream, Single Stream,
Wash me clean, Single Stream.

Thank you for Reading

In Book VI *Amusement Park*, in the final scene, the main character is playing poker with The Man in the Red Hat. They have gone all in, and with everything on the line, they both turn over the same hand: 5 Aces?!

There has been a fifth ace all along, and we realize we haven't been playing with a full deck - ever. So, what is the fifth suit and how does it change the way we play the game of life?

Tarot is an ancient game like playing cards. The exception is Tarot has 22 additional trump cards which symbolize major themes and archetypes. Regular suited cards are lesson cards, helping us understand the game of life. Each suit stands for one of the four elements of water, air, earth and fire.

With the fifth ace, MysterE created a tarot card deck to explore 14 new cards with the suit of New Earth representing the spirit element or compassion. His friends represent the characters in the game, and their likeness is used in the cards themselves.

Up next is a series of books recounting MysterE's life stories through *Black Sheep Tarot – the Game We Already Know*. The characters and lessons come alive, to reveal a hilarious and sobering view of our awakening, plus exploring collectively coming together in the time of our greatest need.

Thank you for reading Single Stream, and we look forward to all being together in the Black Sheep Tarot books.

The Ball of Light

After I wrote the Evolutionary Guidebook in 2010, I met a man my age, who would become a great friend, mentor and guide.

He had his way of being admirable. In the last few years of his life after raising two children, this *young* man established a spiritual center, met his soulmate and married. At his center, *The Alchemy of Innocence*, he shared *presence*, and in that, helped me and many others considerably.

I married Travis and Angee on May 12, 2019, and hosted his memorial service when he left his body on May 12, 2021.

He used to describe the awakening process as unwinding a ball of light. Perhaps it is meaningful for you. *In my words:*

All is frequency. In life, experiencing moment after moment, we are in effect, winding up a ball of light as we would yarn. Each moment is a single point of light in an endless string of light, joining all moments from all lifetimes. It is wound up as we live unaware, until the process reverses itself.

When we awaken, the ball of light begins to unwind, throwing back into our world the energetic frequency of what we left unresolved with guilt and shame. In the unwinding, the frequency of what we thought we got away with is exposed and attracts similar situations, so we can make peace and forgive.

When we awaken, we expect our spiritual work is done. The truth is – it has only just begun. We must resolve with love then, all unfinished business by sharing our gift of presence with all we know. The gift is always love and certainly forgiveness.

Thank you, Denali, for everything. I know you are smiling.

Other Books by MysterE

Single Stream   *Eyes of the Master*

Book I "Ride the Vision of Your Life" (2001) Out of print.

Book II "The Evolutionary Guidebook" (2010 / 2017)

A simple book containing the vibrational coding and instructions on how to shift reality quickly. A must read.

Book III "ReFrame" (2013)

A book about forgiveness and reframing perspective.

Book IV "Give Her What She Wants" (2014) How to use linguistic intelligence and release control to regain our sovereign power in the Age of Feminine Leadership.

Book V "The Gift is Listening" (2016) Enlightened Relationship Guide for Men. Written in 111 short poems.

Book VI "Amusement Park" (2018). A shamanic journey into the heart of a gigantic labyrinth which accelerates ego death and initiates ascension. Revelation of how Black Sheep are the *Chosen Ones* to create New Earth. *Written in all rhyme.*

Book VII "EaseUp Life is Heart" (2019) Poetry. Out of print

Book VIII Spark" (2021) How to repair the mind from heartbreak, betrayal and loss. In rhyme and includes daily prayers.

Book IX "Deal With It Now" (2022). How to vibrationally align with what wants to happen and ascend to New Earth with true forgiveness. In rhyme, making light of dark times.

Books X, XII, XIII & XIV are a part of series entitled: *Black Sheep Tarot: The Game We Already Know.* Coming (2026)

Heart Rocks
In the Trees of Sedona

These rocks find MysterE along the trails. Placing them in the nearest suitable tree and taking *one photo*, he leaves the rocks. So, each photo is unique.

Collected in January - March 2025.
100's of photographs @ agent444.com

Glossary

96 Way - **29**
69 Way - Labyrinth - **30**
Advancement - **34**
All is Provided 4 Now - **94**
Ancient Ones – 43
Blueprints - **14**
Butterfly Effect - **69**
Call for Love - **59**
Choiceless Choice - **30**
Compassion Economy - **81**
Compassion 83
Depth of Seduction - **17**
Desire Field - **18**
Desire The Only Way - **20**
Different is the Same - **31**
Dowsing Rod - **64**
Earth is Calling - **66**
Earth School of Love - **25**
Entrainment - **65**
Eyes of the Master - **26**
Forgiveness - **76**
Free Will - **33**
Fragmentation - **17**
Gap in the Flash - **58**
Giving Up All Battles - **41**
Gliding Past Reactivity - **60**
God's Thought's - **14**
Going Vertical - **95**
Hold the Vision - **41**
Horizontal Plane - **93**
Imagine - **37**
Imagine for a Moment - **92**
Isn't it Obvious? - **90**
Labyrinths (The Way) - **28**
Labyrinth 4 Humanity - **87**
Lesson of the Gap – **68**

Lesson of the Way - **62**
Mass Forgiveness - **76**
Master's Eyes - **26**
Mazes (Which Way?) - **27**
Neutrality - **32**
New Earth - **13**
New Vision - **77**
NowHere - **43**
One Problem Only - **35**
One Simple Action - **99**
Our Addiction - **13**
Our Destiny - **43**
Point of No Return - **54**
Prepared for… Next? - **79**
Purification - **19**
Purpose of Relations - **101**
Relationship - **101**
Resistance Field - **18**
Satisfaction - **12**
Separated Thoughts - **16**
Self-Organizing - **65**
School of Love - **25**
Single Stream - **14**
Single Stream Falls - **62**
Spiritually Advanced - **40**
Sustained Effort - **16**
The Lesson - **62**
True Vision / Sacrifice - **47**
Trust The Process - **41**
Vertical Energy – **95**
Way Showers - **23**
We Already Know - **100**
Well, What is Next? - **79**
Willingness - **35**
Willingness For Change - **98**
Yin Yang - **29**

www.ingramcontent.com/pod-product-compliance
Lightning Source LLC
Chambersburg PA
CBHW071451160426
43195CB00013B/2084